OLD BROADS WAXING POETIC

Compiled by

Julie Kemp Pick

&

Susan Flett Swiderski

Cover design by Michael di Gesu © 2014
http://writing-art-and-design.blogspot.com/

Cover image *Forever Young* by
Francesco Romoli © 2012

ISBN- 13 978-1500642808
ISBN- 10 1500642800

Table of Contents

3

The Crew From A Broad

It began with a cat. After I read Susan Flett Swiderski's "Silly Little Poem," starring a cat trapped in a tree, I knew I found my partner in rhyme. Soon we donned blue wigs, and created Old Broads Waxing Poetic.

I would like to thank Susan for her patience, strength, and wisdom. Like a great coach, **Susan Flett Swiderski** always went above and beyond for the good of the team, and only called this player out when she really needed it.

Joanne Faries also came through for us by graciously formatting all of our poetry. Remarkably, she even had time to add some great poems of her own. Thank you for working tirelessly for our worthwhile cause.

Another round of applause goes to **Francesco Romoli** and **Michael Di Gesu** who magically made our vision sing with their wonderful cover. Francesco created the stunning cover image, while Michael expertly crafted the cover design. Thank you both for helping us make an invaluable first impression.

Without further ado, I'd like to introduce the brilliant bevy of Old Broads:

Connie Biltz, OH – Connie has a wonderful way of writing about her family. Connie's poem about her two sons, "New Arrival," especially hit close to home for me.

Robyn Alana Engel, CA – Robyn was our cheerleading captain. She helped us recruit some of our wonderful talent, and her loving spirit really shines through in her versatile array of poetry.

Fran Fischer, CA – Fran's exceptional sense of humor has risen to new levels. The talented writer even managed to turn her personal battle with breast cancer into a comedic masterpiece.

Delores Lowndes, CAN – Delores has an amazing lightness in her writing. She has the ability to pull words out of a hat, and make them dance on the page.

Liza Carens Salerno, MA – Liza can bring to life breathtaking imagery one moment, and pen a heartfelt message to her daughter the next.

Thanks to our talented group of Old Broads for pouring their hearts into this meaningful project. A special thanks also goes out to you for buying this book to help benefit the remarkable CARE organization. Our hope is that you'll laugh, cry, or smile along with us, as getting older is easier when you're not alone.

Julie

Labor of Love

Age is just a number,
A fact both trite and true;
If you look beyond our sags and bags,
You may learn something new.
Being slower to remember
Doesn't mean that we are dumb;
Our brains bulge with perspective
Of the past, and things to come.
Experience has been our teacher;
And humor, our saving grace.
Aging may not be a piece of cake,
But there's a smile upon our face.
With its highs, lows, twists, and turns,
Life's given us quite a ride,
But in spite of the wrinkly bodies you see,
We still feel young inside.
We're old; we're bold,
And we have a lot to share.
You know why we bother?
Because we truly CARE.

Okay, okay, okay, so it isn't too likely that you're
gonna learn anything earth-shattering in the
pages of our little poetry book, but you may

gain some insight and get a few laughs by looking at life through our droopy-lidded eyes.

And yes, we do care. That's why all proceeds from the sale of this book are going to CARE International, an organization that has been delivering hope and a helping hand to people all over the world since 1945.

This group of old broads from the U.S. and Canada hope you enjoy our work. It's been an honest-to-goodness labor of love.

Susan

Connie Biltz

Connie Biltz is a writer and poet. Her essays and stories have been published in *Seventeen, Sunshine, On Campus, Working Writer,* and *Cats Magazine,* among others. She writes a poetry blog called *More Where That Came From* which can be found at www.conniebiltz.com. Some of her other poems appeared in the book, *Musings 2013.* She lives in Akron, Ohio with her husband John. They have two grown sons, Chris and Andy.

Sidewalk Stories

Traces of yellow chalk dust--
remains of a hopscotch game.
 One, two, hop, jump.
Pick up the stone.
Play with a friend,
or play alone.

Uneven concrete,
cracked and lifted by gnarled roots
in the shady spot under the old elm tree,
where walkers trip or stub a toe,
and roller skaters fall
and scrape a knee.

Lovers stroll
 as the sun sets.
"*Hold my hand.*
Come walk with me."
She leans into his shoulder.
He rests his cheek against her hair.
Such a thrill to hold her.
A day, such as this,
he thought he'd never see.

Two elderly sisters,
arm in arm they walk along,
one keeps her balance with a cane.
Both widowed and left behind,
trying to fight the loneliness,
just holding on, trying to stay sane.
They fill their days with emptiness,
wondering why, wondering when.
So many questions still remain.

An exhausted mom
pushes her baby's stroller,
hoping the motion
will lull him to sleep.
He nods off and drops his pacifier.
It's surprising
as we walk along;
the things we find,
the things we lose,
the things we keep

Raggedy Anne

My mom made the doll with love.
She made it while thinking of me.
A comforting friend, that Raggedy Anne,
and *always* good company.

She knotted the orange yarn hair.
She stitched the nose and eyes.
She sewed on the rick-rack and striped socks,
and measured the pinafore for size.

I told Raggedy all of my secrets.
She promised never to tell.
She was quiet and wise and patient,
and she knew me, oh so well.

My mom made the doll with love.
She made it while thinking of me.
A comforting friend, that Raggedy Anne,
and *always* good company.

Today is my mom's birthday.
I miss her—she's on my mind.
I take comfort in the love she shared with me
in the things she left behind.

Lilacs and Love

"Nothing says spring like a lilac breeze,"
Mom closed her eyes, smiled, and sighed.
The scent would come drifting in,
with curtains billowing and windows wide.

My mother gathered them by the armful,
bunches of lilac blooms with a fragrance that
was heaven sent.
She took them to my grandma *every* Mother's
Day,
sharing her love, showing her gratitude,
knowing how much it meant.

She loved lilacs too, my mother did,
and she was glad we had plenty to spare.
It doubled her joy for them, I think,
knowing she was able to share.

Grandma would bury her nose in the lilacs,
and breathe in the heady scent too.
She arranged them carefully in a milk glass vase,
and there was one thing I *always* knew.

Grandma loved me, and my mom did too,
so fierce and wide and deep.
Remembering those lilacs they shared
is a memory I'll always keep.
Forever the sight of a lilac bush,
or the hint of its fragrance in the air,
will remind me of those two ladies before me,
who had lilacs and love to spare.

A Weighty Question

Those ladies at the door,
manning the Weight Watchers scale,
say encouraging words if I do well,
or sympathize with me, if I fail.

The leaders are there
teaching me new ways to cope
and filling me up
with inspiration and hope.

I've counted all my points,
and I've done my exercise.
My clothes are looser!
I'm down another size!!

If I have a loss to report,
the leaders send up a CHEER
because losers WIN at *this* sport.
"HURRAY!!" they say.
"There's *less* of you here!"

(Wait that seems a little strange.
Do they want me to...disappear?)

16

Just Call Me Curly

I'm trying to make up my mind,
Just a trim or an all-new style?
Make it short? Let it grow?
I waver and then give in to whim,
Saying, "Oh what the heck, let's give it a go."

Tiffany, the stylist, asks,
"So what are we thinking today?"
(I'm thinking that Tiffany is much too thin,
And that a cheeseburger might do her some
good.
And look how young she is!
How old *is* she, anyway?)

But, of course,
One can't say such things,
even though one might think them.
So I say, "I don't know.
Maybe add some layers,
and give the ends a trim."

She begins clipping and snipping,
combing, measuring, spritzing.
Then I feel her make that first short chop,
and I know things have gone too far,
but it's too late, too late to yell, "NO! STOP!"

So I hold my breath for a moment,
and cringe a little inside.
Already thinking about damage control--
Gel, mousse, curling iron?

17

Perhaps a big hat in which to hide?
I wonder if she'll ever finish.
She cuts and cuts some more.
I glance down and feel a little sick inside,
When I see how much hair is on the floor!

At last she is finished.
She spins me around in my chair.
She smiles, hands me a mirror,
and says, "There now. Do you like your new
hair?"

I take a peek and see curls gone wild.
They are soft and tumbling,
But much too high.
I don't recognize the face I see.
To my old self, I say, "Goodbye."

I tell my family, "Perhaps it will be all right.
Once I calm it down with my comb."
"You look pretty."
"I like it. Hey, it looks nice,"
Say those kind fellows back at home.

Of course, those guys
Have to live with me,
So they know the right thing to say.
And though, I'm not quite used to it *yet*,
I'm adjusting,
And I take comfort in knowing,
That it's just hair anyway,
And it really will grow back.
It will. IT WILL…someday.

Backyard Camping

Ropes, poles, and canvas,
when wrangled by two young boys,
wriggle in an awkward dance,
to the music of their raucous noise.

It takes enormous effort,
but a tent finally appears in the yard.
They share high fives and kudos,
saying, "See, that wasn't so hard."

Roasting hot dogs and making s'mores,
gets the night off to a good start.
They've gathered popcorn, sleeping bags,
flashlights.
They're telling stories--feeling smart.

But darkness settles in,
and the night feels lonely and long.
The ground is hard, lumpy, and cold,
and everything seems so wrong.

Mosquitoes buzz by one boy's ear.
A spider tickles the other one's arm.
The neighbor's dog snuffles outside.
"Oh no! Is that a bear?"
"SOUND THE ALARM!"
(Camping out in the back yard
was *quickly* losing its charm.)

"Do you want to go back inside?"
They say in unison to one another.

They scurry out of the tent,
grateful for the back porch light,
left shining by their mother.

Never were two boys so happy,
to be tucked in safely into their beds,
with warm blankets pulled up to their chins,
and soft pillows under their heads.

It was the first time for them to learn,
(with many more instances yet to be).
That the dream is sometimes *better* than reality,
and everything's perfect in a fantasy.

New Arrival

Once he was *our* new arrival,
scrawny, tiny, and pink
next to his big brother.
Another face, another link.

He was the last piece of the puzzle.
He made our family complete.
He had his Momma's smile
(but he had his Daddy's feet.)

He's no baby anymore, of course.
Although he once sat upon my knee,
now he reaches things on the top shelf
and hands them *down* to me.

A letter came from the university
welcoming *their* new arrivals to the school.
He will soon be joining *them*.
Passing time can be so cruel.

Older brother has moved away.
Our household now numbers three,
but before long, there will be just two
in our shrinking family tree.

We are all of us coming and going
with the arrival of each new day.
Trying to find where we are supposed to be.
Trying to find our way.

I guess it's his turn to buy a ticket.

He has the big, wide world to greet.
I take comfort in knowing he'll do it
while wearing his Momma's smile
and walking with his Daddy's feet.

Straight Line Winds

I remember picking grapes,
twisting them off the vine and into a silver
bowl.
My sons were playing in the yard.
running about, throwing rocks into a hole.

None of us saw it coming.
It came upon us so fast.
It was oddly quiet.
The sky, bruised, an uneasy, purple cast.

The first gust came from nowhere.
The purple sky had turned to black.
"GET INSIDE! GET INSIDE!" I yelled.
The wind whipped around us and we ran,
terrified, not looking back.

We slammed through the doors
and thundered down the stairs,
huddled together for a moment,
taken unawares.

Catching our breath and safe,
we peered in awe
at what was happening outside.
Then we all gasped at once
as we saw the fronts collide.

A row of trees snapped in half
one by one like dominoes
in the yard where my sons

had *just* been playing.
What might have happened?
Only Heaven knows.

We watched, mesmerized,
as the wind took its toll.
Branches crashing down
over the rock-filled hole.

"Not a tornado, not a twister,"
said the weatherman next day,
"just straight line winds
that knocked down everything in the way."

When I saw the path of destruction
littered across our yard,
I offered up a prayer of thanks,
and my sons yelped and squirmed
because I hugged them extra hard.

Turn Down the Silence

Sleeping on the couch,
spouse and poodle snore in tandem,
while the clock ticks away on the wall.
In the kitchen,
whooshes and hums from the dishwasher
softly dance in rhythm
and float their way down the hall.
From the basement,
the clothes dryer rumbles and thumps
while the clothes washer creaks in a spin.
Air whistling
through the vent by the floor
keeps me warm,
as the furnace kicks on
yet again.
Outside,
the January wind is howling,
but it's mostly quiet here within.
Gone are the boisterous sounds
of two little boys.
No toy trucks, no squabbles, no video games.
No exuberant din.
The silence is so much louder *now*
than their clank and clamor *ever* was...
back then.

Kitchen Memories

When I think about her kitchen,
I can still see her in it,
up to her elbows, kneading bread,
flour rising in little puffs from the counter,
while she punched and folded the ball of dough.
She'd let it rise then in a glass bowl.
It was white on the inside;
the outside was striped in red.
She'd cover the bowl with a dish towel.
"Why do you do that?" I asked.
"That will keep it warm," she said.
Sunny yellow curtains were hanging
on the windows above the sink.
Her view, our back yard:
the old maple tree was straight ahead.
Off to the right, the swing set where we played.
Off to the left, irises, tulips, and peonies in the
flower bed.
She'd half sing and half hum to herself
the song that had played the day she was wed.
"I love you truly, truly dear."
And when I remember her sweet voice,
hear it playing softly in my head,
I wonder what kitchen memories
my sons will have of me--
in the heart of our home
where problems were solved,
parties were planned,
and prayers were said.
Will they remember coloring Easter eggs,
baking brownies, and cutting out sugar cookies?

26

I hope they remember most the love and the
fun we had,
and the good feelings that came from having a
family
where our hearts were full and our bellies were
well-fed.

Your Words

Be careful with your words.
Watch which ones you say,
or they may come back to haunt you
in an unsuspecting way.

Your words can be a weapon.
Your words can be a tool.
Your words can make you look quite wise
or like the biggest fool.

Choose them very carefully.
Choose who hears them too.
Give your word to those you trust,
and they'll be true to you.

Your words can trip you up
if you've strung them into lies.
Your words will sometimes contradict
what you're saying with your eyes.

Words can help you share your love
or reveal a deep desire.
Your words can incite a riot,
break a heart, or inspire.

Your words can be a comfort;
help to soothe, calm, and heal.
Your words can be an oath,
a vow to seal the deal.

If the words you choose to use
are the kindest you can find,
you'll never wish to take them back;
erase, delete, or hit rewind.

Robyn Alana Engel

Robyn Alana Engel, a native Californian, is best known for her humorous dating anecdotes. Her writing, though, crosses a variety of genres. In 2012, Robyn published a poetry book, *Just the Right Time*. She's also been published in *Being Single Magazine*, the *Chico News and Review*, and the *Journal of Jewish Communal Services*. In April of 2014, Robyn won a writing contest hosted by www.midlifecollage.com. Through it all, Miss Engel shamelessly boasts about her chocoholism. When Robyn isn't thinking about chocolate, she can be found eating chocolate while blogging at Life by Chocolate, www.Rawknrobyn.blogspot.com. She apologizes for any chocolate smudges here or elsewhere.

Ode to the Oreo

Oh Nabisco
Why'd you go
And desecrate the Oreo?
I liked it fine before the change
To an array of flavors gross and strange.
With double stuff, you should have quit.
But birthday cake?
Who'd eat that sh*t?
You're triple stacked
And berry burst. Neapolitan.
And it got worse.
You hit new lows with the words "low fat."
What PR guru thought of that?
Nabisco, tell me, why'd you go
And make a "springtime" Oreo
That's dyed in freaky loud yellow?
Could that be cream or real bright snow?
You've gone peanut butter and mint too.
A Girl Scout rip-off -- Shame on you!
So Oreo, now I must go.
It's you, not me, if you must know.
You gave good licks and chews to start.
But Big Fig Newton's my new tart.

31

Diamonds

Bring back the days of simple things
Of diamond-shaped, sweet candy rings.
Truth or Dare, you dared not lie.
Tick-Tac-Toe, we'd always tie.
The rich and poor got cootie shots
Wars were won, when they weren't fought.

Saturday cartoons were best.
Lick the frosting, ditch the rest.
We skipped to school without a care
And Underoos were fun to wear.

To see your friends, you went to class
And pulled your pants above your ass.
I was Van Gough with my Lite Brite
And Jordache had the fit that's right.

When talent mattered
Kindness pleased.
We swung on tires, hung from trees.
A rock was skipped and made a pet
Tails or scissors won the bet.

Bring back the days of simple things
Kaleidoscopes and cheap mood rings.
Gumby walked through any book.
How would he navigate the Nook?

Scary meant a horror flick
Not bullets sprayed by someone sick.
A touch was always warm and right.

Hope paved the way
When days brought night.

Now, money talks and makes the rules.
So-called actors, obscene fools.
Bieber's stoned but Lohan's clean.
Disney stars, sinful and mean.

Reign in the days of simple things
The cherished gems a moment brings.
Through children's eyes
The time is here
For simple things to vast appear

Courage

Extending the dance, when you've long lost
your groove
Swimming to shore too frail to move.

Stepping towards light, when darkness abounds
Permitting a laugh amid no other sounds.
Confronting a beast no one should endure
It strikes with no warning, no reprieve and no
cure.

Snuggling with hope, when the pain you can't
bear
Unveiling your heart in the face of despair.

Conveying a smile, when you'd much rather cry
Speaking the truth though it's safer to lie.

Taking a stance, when integrity's lost
Forcing what's right in spite of the cost.

Holding to faith in your value and worth
Maintaining a grace that softens the earth.

Passing with ease
As you air your last breath

A hero whose soul
Transcends life
and death.

Something

Sometimes we reach for something
but it's something we can't see
When a moment feels like hours,
And we struggle to just be.
Despair is all-consuming
And what's next is what we fear.
We listen hard for something
Uncertain what we'll hear.
Sometimes we pray for something,
but lack religious creed.
When all it takes is something
And with it, we are freed.

I'm glad you are that something
 when something's what I need.

We Wish We Could

Shattered hearts
Broken dreams
A desperate world
In which it seems
Nothing unfolds the way it should
To change the facts
We wish we could
So life makes sense
And children thrive
Angels prevail
While demons die
Hate is squelched yet understood
To change the facts
 We wish we could.
To change the facts, we wish we could.

Everything and Nothing

We grapple to find reasons

When there are none to be found

Since hatefulness and evil

Never stem from somewhere sound

We want to make wrong right somehow

But can't undo the pain

Of spirits crushed by tragedy

Mere words seem so inane

We can offer loving kindness

To those who fight to live

It's everything.

It's nothing.

It's all we have to give.

How far we have gone?

How far we have gone
How much movement we've made
When text isn't a book
But a means to get laid

And those who offend
We simply unfriend

How far have we gone
How much did we gain
When a tag is for photos
And a tweet, the inane?

When we "like" a good joke
Say "hey" with a poke?

How far we have gone
To go viral we aim
Gotta increase the numbers
And stay in the game

How far have we gone?

Mere Chance

I stride into your eyes and see
I could be you.
You could be me.
Divided lives that crave the same:
Love, respect, a valued name.
Bereft of excess,
our needs so few:
Awaking safe
with breath anew.
Both good souls,
two lots to bear.
Would life make sense,
a fate we'd share.
Yet I bathe myself
in waste replete
As you stave demons
on the street.
Your time,
a fight
and mine,
a dance.
Mere chance contrasts
each circumstance.

Your hurdles, vast
Your earnest, true

How easily
I could be you.

Worth the Sad

I think I know
It's worth the sad

The taste of bliss
That I once had

Playful madness, tickle fests
My trusting cheek against his chest.

A lovers' cove, a future planned.
Wedding vows, the world in hand.

I lived my dream.
With faith, I flew. To him my all
A promise true.

He snapped and shredded
Us apart
Confusion, tears
A fearful heart

From glee to dismal
In a blink

It's worth the sad

I know

I think

If I Die Young

If I die young or an old shrew
Keep a smile for me, another for you.

Laugh out loud when it's right
Bathe in tears when it's wrong
Dance with ants in your pants
When you can't stand the song.

If I die young or an old shrew
Keep a smile for me, another for you.

Publish my writing, all credit to me.
Produce my life story with Sarah J.P.*
A bold, brawny hottie will play my main squeeze
Any looker will do. No Scientologists, please!

If I die young or an old shrew
Keep a smile for me, another for you.

Devour fair-trade chocolate
When life's sour or sweet
Catch hope in your heart and
Spring in your feet

If I die young or an old shrew
Keep a smile for me, another for you.

*Sarah Jessica Parker or, if you'd rather,
Jennifer Aniston

Divinity

A child with a lisp
An awkward first kiss
Laughter that hurts and
Hiccups in spurts
A teen who's been jilted
A pink rose that's wilted
An 'ole clunker that runs
Hot dogs without buns
A surgeon who smiles
A friend who's in need
A spider that scurries
Once it's been freed
A kid who asks "Why?"
A mommy's bold cry.
The last piece of chocolate
Left in the box
Polka dots and plaid garments
And Tevas with socks.
A Dixie cup filled with low-end red wine
Goosebumps up the arms
What could be more divine?

Back in the Day

Back in the day
We meant you and me.
To feel was to touch.
To touch set you free.

Courage and valor defined one as great -
Not being a whiney, crazed parent of eight.

When actors could act,
Performers could sing,
Reality shows starred Carson and Bing.

Back in the day,
Mail came to your door.
Wrappers bore gifts.
You walked to the store.

Ice cream trucks stopped on the corner street.
Fifteen cent big sticks, a most awesome treat.

Nice girls didn't google, switch users or tweet.
Blackberries were juicy and raspberries, sweet.

Nice guys didn't sag, log off or shut down.
When sex was sacred, and text, just a noun.

Back In the day, botox was unknown.
Surgery was for illness,
Cocktails for the grown.

Cells made up blood.
Breakfast, with Tang.
TVs had antennas, and
Telephones rang.

Back in the day,
You ne'er felt hella rad
When your BFF told you
Your outfit looked bad.
I.M. meant I am.
To chat meant to talk.
You swam with you tube,
And teachers used chalk.

Back in the day,
A Chevrolet brought you clout.
Cowboys re-booted before stepping out.

Blue tooth was concerning.
Hot meant close to burning.

Fruit smoothies were exotic.
Laptops, erotic.

Back in the day,
Old school was a house.
A pad for a bachelor,
And cheese for a mouse.

Word!
I'm sayin'
Feel me, and don't weep.

Oprah continues to represent the peep (for
another minute).

And back in the day, who'd ever dream
That a Black man would hold the office
Supreme.

We go backwards and forwards,
Forwards and then back,
In circles, and sideways,
But land up on track.

Back in the day...
We means you and me.

Joanne Faries

Joanne Faries, originally from the Philadelphia area, lives in Texas with her husband Ray. She considers herself fortunate to be able to pursue a writing hobby/career (the title fluctuates) after eons in the business world.

Published in *Doorknobs & Bodypaint*, Joanne writes short stories, flash fiction, and poetry.

Joanne is proud of her independently published books: **My Zoo World (If All Dogs Go to Heaven, Then I'm in Trouble), Wordsplash Flash**, and three **Wordsplash Poetry Puddle** collections: *Nature, Tread Water,* and *Hazy Memories.* All are available on Amazon.

Finally, she enjoys reading and movies, and is the film critic for the *Little Paper of San Saba* (a town without a cinema)

Check out her blog: www.wordsplash-joannefaries.blogspot.com

engulfed

in memory
enveloped in cream colored
afghan cloud
grandmother crocheted love
gnarled finger
legacy

bouquet dropped

park entrance curb
no mournful curled leaves
white daisies
gleamed in memory

Mexican Petunias

crumpled brown stalks
faltered after freeze
ice smothered, they collapsed
no memory of purple posies
withered bleak garden
wind rustled
hunkered slumber

Movie Snow

glistens, pristine white glow
contrasts with nubby tree bark
red scarves wound around necks
blue mittens packing snow balls
muffled hush blankets cars
woodpiles, bikes left outdoors
smothered in crystalline splendor
movie snow frosts panes as
laughter ripples over hot chocolates
fireplace crackle, and winter nap

Tango salsa heavy metal beat

my tin ear, lead feet refuse
defeat. Snap fingers
and sway to the tunes I hear
heart soars with a ballad
growls with bass lines
grooves to Philly soul
air guitar with the best
nab Grammy for best shower
solo ever

Lazy

reclined sofa languish
she contemplated entertainment
eyes swept the room and closed
slowed breath, she pondered

Sunday

let minutes linger
clock tick, inaction resounds
relinquish responsibility
light snore

surprise me

turn of phrase
sound snippet
color splash
motion whirr
upbeat tempo

wake me from my reverie
beckon, break the ennui
paper shuffle routine

run rampant
douse doldrums
savory aromas
chocolate dollop
tease temptation

sneak a kiss

Corporate divorce

work heart palpitations
dry mouth, forehead squeezed tensions
build. Owner returned from trip
home closets cleaned, office bare,
forty year wife waved goodbye

employee questions
security, money, jobs
boss' manic actions, hushed phone calls
nervous paper shuffle
she shall squeeze almighty dollar

we're the kids
in the custody battle
latch key shelter
alarm code function
future unknown

Love assessment

nothing like a long term couple's imploded
marriage

it reverts to me, my, our, and we look in the
mirror
for symptoms of divorce disease
cover our mouths and bite back bitter retorts
eat meals together , turn off phones, and watch
expressions, smile, ask questions, discuss the
day
share inside jokes, plan a trip, and nuzzle
extra few minutes after alarm

our love is the antidote

first day

varies year to year dependent on weather
rainy cool nights bring the chill
postpone the expectations
pool lounge laziness

first day cloudless, slight breeze
kids run/walk to diving board
minimal bounce hurls them shrieking
arm flail, half tuck, cannonball burbles

she saunters to shallow end, dips the toe
lowers one step, and another
pale legs shimmer, as she oozes
breath intake as slight splash cools

small of the back
she initiates plunge immersion
emerges renewed, winter memory erased
adjusts bathing strap, leans back to float

first day of summer declared

Beach Day Rhythm

early morning, they arrange chairs
same place, ten feet from a lifeguard
a semi-circle around an ice chest

squat leathery women in
skirted flowery swimsuits
strained at the bosom
scurry about like full-breasted seagulls

mothers squawk at tanned children
who tote buckets of water to
castle creations

lilting Italian accents a
vicious game of bocce ball
old men in trunks, brown socks,
and sandals shuffle past the women

grandmothers stand dimpled knees deep
armfuls of gleeful toddlers dipped
legs and toes curl upwards
escape from cold lapping waves

teens beg for money
pizza, fries, and ice cream
shrill arcade bells call them
to the boardwalk

late afternoon, chairs collapsed
towels snapped
sand brushed from chubby legs
men, women, and children stagger
to beach home showers

incoming tide erases
seagulls swoop, land, and chatter

Previous published in *Storyteller* – December
2008

Mimic

peel thin string
attached to cellophane
flip box lid
tear open shiny wrapper
tap box
shake out
single white stick
rub under nose
      inhale
between two fingers
curl, not squeeze
bring to puckered lips
      squint
pause, tongue tease
teeth tidbit
tilt head
linger, remove
      flick
sidelong glance
      exhale

      wait
      wait

smoke wafts, dissipates
      repeat
Dad's post-dinner Camel
my dessert candy cigarette

Previously published in *Blue Fifth Review* – Fall 2008

Fran Fischer

Fran was born in 1934, which she figures makes her about three years older than dirt. She has lived her entire life in Los Angeles, CA. She and her husband of 59+ years have lived in the same house since 1961--it's just the gypsy in their souls. They have left their nest to travel extensively, mostly in the US and Europe. She says her favorite vacation was to the Galapagos Islands where her husband sat down to rest on on what he thought was a large rock. When it moved, he realized it was a quite large and fortunately docile sea lion. She has crossed everything off her bucket list except a trip to Mt. Rushmore. For her 74th birthday she took a zero gravity flight, like the astronaut's "vomit comet", and flew like Superman while on board.

She has been published in "Open Doors: Fractured Fairy Tales" and some other anthologies, the names of which she can't recall, but she *does* remember that her debut book, "Fishducky's Fables", is available on Amazon. Her blog, "fishducky, finally" can be found at fishducky.blogspot.com and is published twice weekly.

GOODBYE, LEFT BREAST
(ODE TO A MASTECTOMY)

I just thought I'd like to say goodbye
As you go to that medical waste disposal in the
sky.
Say hi to my tonsils and have no fears.
We'll all get back together in a few years.

You've known me the seventy-nine years of my
life.
You saw me as a teen, and then a wife.
Your first job was attracting men
And next you were a breastaurant for my
children.
When the doors of the milkbar finally closed
You went back to a purely decorative mode.
Which was fine, until last week
When you (and other parts) became antique.
I no longer attract young men of twenty,
But that's all right, because I've had plenty.
And as for that other use, well, we all know
The odds of me nursing again are low.
But it's in my nature to be a little sappy,
And with or without you I'll keep on being
happy.
Most would count this a loss when it comes to
my score.
Will I miss you? A little. Do I need you? No
more!
I will be losing some symmetry,
On this I think we can both agree.

I may tilt to one side as I walk through town
But I'll try to adjust and not fall down.

Yet I'm not through having fun
And lifting my face to the warmth of the sun.
And being with friends and laughing (I'll show
you)
So ta ta, left ta-ta, it was nice to know you!

*I wrote this, obviously, when I was 73.
~~Every word~~ ~~Most of it~~ Some of it is
true.
Years 74-79 haven't seen much
improvement.*

AN ODE TO BEING SEVENTY-THREE

My legs are sore. I need a cane.
My body has gone quite insane.
My breasts were perky as a song.
My bra size now is 40-Long.

I cannot hear. I cannot see.
I have to pee. Oh, woe is me!
My body's fat. My skin is thin.
I do not like the shape I'm in.

I cough–I cough until I choke.
I'm going out to have a smoke.
My bones are brittle, I fear my fate.
I'm liable to disintegrate.

My memory now seems to have gone.
Who is that standing on my lawn?
It's my husband Bud–or is his name Paul?
I thought he died–I can't recall.

61

The thermometer says it's 63.
I don't know why it lies to me.
I can't stop sweating—watch me pour.
My body says it's 104.

My joints creak and pop so bad
I'm like a steel drum from Trinidad.
Leg cramps woke me again last night.
Why is my skin so loose and my muscles tight?

My health is iffy. I may not thrive.
But life is good—and I'm still alive!
And yet I wonder more and more
What I'll be like at seventy-four!

~~ODE TO~~ OWED BY BEING 80

Dear Age—

When you started borrowing and rearranging,
I really didn't mind.
You took my slim flat stomach
But added lots to my behind.
You even took my memory so
I wouldn't notice things,
Like my slender upper arms,
Which have now developed wings.
You gave me my own road map,
But why put it on my face?
Couldn't you at least have found
A less conspicuous place?

My throat, swanlike and slim,
Which I had always thought'll
Stay that way, you decided to
Change to a turkey wattle.

How can I forget that the boobs of my youth,
Which once I let live free,
Are conveniently able, now,
To rest upon my knee?

My hair was a lovely chocolate brown
And is now a faded grey,
Unless I let my hairdresser
Bi-monthly have her way.

How nice of you that on my hands

63

You have given me age spots,
So when I'm bored I can play a game;
It's called "Connect the Dots".

You've put a tremor in those hands,
My steadiness I'm losing,
But I must admit, saves a step when I pour
Stuff that says, "Shake before using."

I used to be able to work all day
And party 'til the sun shone bright.
Please tell me, when did 6:00 p.m.
Become the new midnight?

Lunch now comes at 9:00 a.m.
And dinner around 3.
I have breakfast before I go to bed.
I've reorganized, you see.

No one has hit on me for years,
A fact that's sad but true.
I'd love to hug and kiss some guys
(And whatever else I used to do).

I could charm any man or boy,
Thought that would always be my fate.
Who knew that my charms would come
With an expiration date?

You took my young stud of a husband
And made him almost 83,
I'm still young (in my mind, at least);
Now he's too old for me!

My bones have become quite brittle
And my skin is paper thin.
I'm shorter than I used to be.
I blame you for the shape I'm in!

I thought I'd accepted getting old,
Though in my heart of hearts,
I'd really like to be young again
But I can no longer get the parts.

You took these things without permission
And I deeply feel their lack,
So all these things you "borrowed",
You owe me and I want them back!

THE WOULD-BE POET

I'm telling you quite honestly
        I'd love to write fine poetry.
I'd show such versatility
        that everyone would honor me.
The words would come forth trippingly
        as if they had a melody.
I'd write of plants; of rose and tree.
        I'd be a big celebrity!
I'd write of kings and royalty
        and I'd discuss humanity.
I'd write of love so wistfully,
        of sadness and of *joie de vie*
And I would do this masterfully.
        I'd lecture universally.
I'd do this work unselfishly
        (though I'd accept gratuities).

So let me add, in summary,
        I'd gain much popularity.
My poems loved so zealously
        that publishers would say to me,
"Write more!" They'd beg me fervently
        for poems to fill their glossaries.
They'd organize parades; you'd see
        me waving at fans jauntily.
The crowds, no longer orderly,
        would clamor with intensity.
The President would say, pleadingly,
        "Our Poet Laureate you have to be!"
I would decline, quite modestly.

This could become insanity.
I'd have to write incessantly,
      If I were to act accordingly.
There would be no more time for me
      to sit and daydream lazily.
I'd be pressured overwhelmingly
      to keep up this activity.
I'd hear "Please write!" repeatedly
      'til writer's cramp took hold of me.
My brain would start to atrophy.
      No one would want to be with me.
My friends, is this my destiny?
      Why, in this great democracy,
Should talent push relentlessly
      and rob me of my dignity?
And so I ask you, tearfully,
      is that the way it has to be
If I could write as beautifully
      as I had wished for previously?
My literary wizardry
      might just attack me fatally!
I've thought this thing out carefully
      and realize the absurdity
Of living my life tragically
      if I could write great poetry.

With apologies to humankind,
      I fear that someday I would find
My nerves all tangled in a bind
      which I, (poor soul) could not unwind,
So—never mind!

A VISIT FROM THE EASTER BUNNY

'Twas the night before Easter, when all
through the house
Not a creature was stirring, not even my
spouse.
The baskets were placed in the yard with
such care,
In hopes that the Easter Bunny soon
would be there.

The children were nestled all snug in
their beds,
While visions of Easter eggs danced in
their heads;
And mamma with her night cream
covering her nose,
Had just settled down for a long
springtime's doze;

When out on the lawn there arose such
a noise,
I jumped up to yell at the neighborhood
boys.
Those kids sounded like they were out
of their minds,
I pulled back the drapes and opened the
blinds.

The moon on the breast of the new
fallen trash
Gave the alley below me a certain
panache,
When, what to my wondering eyes
should be featured,
But a miniature hot rod, and eight tiny
creatures,

With a little old driver, so lively and
funny,
I knew in a moment it must be the
Bunny.

More rapid than eagles his coursers they
came,
And he whistled, and shouted, and
called them by name:

"Now, Dagger! Now, Danger! Now, Ba
dass and Ice!
On, T-Rex! On, Rudeboy! On, Bigfoot
and Slice!
To the top of the porch! Someone toss
me a beer!
Now dash away! Dash away before the
cops can get here!"

As dry leaves that before the wild
hurricane fly,
When they meet with an obstacle,
mount to the sky,
So up to the housetop the coursers they
flew,
With a carload of eggs, and the big
Bunny, too.

And then, in a twinkling, I heard the
roof go kaput
From the prancing and pawing of each
little foot.
As I drew in my head, and was turning
around,
Through the window the Easter Bunny
came in with a bound.

He was dressed all in fur, from his foot
to his ear,
He saw me but showed absolutely no
fear.
A bundle of eggs he had flung on his
back,
And he looked like a peddler just
opening his pack.

His eyes, oh, how bloodshot! He was
sort of scary!
His cheeks were like roses, his nose like a
cherry!
His droll little mouth was drawn up like a
sheep

And he said, "Hey, dude, why aren't you
asleep?"

The stump of a joint he held tight in his
teeth,
And the smoke it encircled his head like
a wreath.
He had a broad face and he was kind of
smelly,
Yet he shook, when he laughed, like a
bowlful of jelly.

He was chubby and plump, a right nasty
old elf,
But I laughed when I saw him, in spite of
myself.
A wink of his eye as he brandished his
piece,
Soon told me I should have called the
police.

He spoke not a word, but went straight
to his work,
And took all my good stuff, then turned,
the big jerk.
He left me the eggs, but who wanted
them now?

And out the window he went, with an
arrogant bow.

He sprang to his hot rod, to his gang gave a whistle,

And away they all flew like the down of a thistle.

But I heard him exclaim, though it was more like a hoot,

"Happy Easter to all, and thanks for the loot!"

Delores Lowndes

Delores is a crotchety, curmudgeonly old lady living out her dotage with her long suffering husband of forty years. Always a writer at heart (I didn't say a GOOD one) she never really got around to expressing herself with pen and ink until she retired from the insurance industry and discovered blogging four years ago. Since then she has been burning rubber catching up on lost time. You can access her blog at: ramblingsoftheterminallyaging.blogspot.com

A Dusty Country Road

long dusty interludes
hair raising peaks and valleys
I race alongside
rail fences
corn crops
dally
in cool dappled shade
of ancient maples
tossing their lacy branches
in summer breezes

names on mailboxes
seldom change here
down long leafy lanes
glimpses of century old houses and barns
can be seen
families at work
less often at play
happy in their
togetherness
their history

long nights of
frog song and cricket dance
the old moon
watching over me
stars whirling overhead
the faint twinkle of lights
down those quiet
shadow shrouded driveways

the only sounds
those of the night
the lowing of a cow
the wail of a coyote

early morning
brings the rattle
of the milk pail
the deep rumble
of giant tractors
preparing
for the work of the day

a lone pickup
eases along
putting mail in mail boxes
a snarling tractor
pulls a laden hay wagon
little boys on bikes
fishing poles and lunches
riders
three abreast
dust rising
from the horses feet

sudden rainfall
creates explosions of dust
patters on leaves overhead
gurgles in the culverts
soothes, refreshes
brings life

to this lonely
country road

Construction

making what is
out of what was
today
out of yesterday
the who I was
and the who I am
making peace
with each other
we're on shaky terms
she and I
but we're working on it

Dusting Day

hesitantly
I approach the daily decay
that drifted
crash landed
on all flat surfaces
not wanting to disturb
the build up of history
dust of kings and commoners
it's gently gathered
returned to the earth
to fly in the wind
God speed

Early Morning Kitchen

So peaceful, the kitchen, in the early hours...
One gone to work,
One still in bed.
Like a tranquil day with no breeze blowing,
Coffee steam rising in a prayer to heaven,
Sun warmed patches of floor,
Clean, gleaming counter tops, cool and
reflective...
A moment of peace before the storm of the
day,
the shipwreck of the evening.

Moving Day

Her house
packed up,
floors
swept clean,
boxes
removed,
memories
neatly packaged
in old letters
and photographs,
mirrors
no longer
reflect her life.
The door opens
and she,
stepping out,
leaves the shell
once occupied
by her soul...
moves on

Missing Pieces

At the entrance
always,
bird bright eyes
focus sharply on the door.
Today, surely today
someone will come.
It's been so long.
When was the last time?
April? May?
Christmas is in the air.
Carols are playing.
Hope is dying.
Frail speckled hands
lie in her lap
empty,
Bone thin ankles
crossed neatly.
Pieces of her puzzle,
her life,
are scattered,
the lid of the box
with the picture
missing.
Is that why no one comes?
They don't know
where they fit in the picture anymore?

My Home Town

Limestone,
chiseled by calloused hand,
now softened by time,
holds its memories fast.
Ancient window frames
bake in the sun,
whisper their stories
through countless layers
of paint.
At the river's edge
willows dip branches
in cool water
where wily trout
lay in wait
for delicate treats of mayfly.
Shouts of children
playing in parks
rise to the sky.
The old ones
comfortable
on worn bleachers
watch the game of the week.
Saturday lawnmowers buzz.
Fragrant smoke from backyard Webers
rises prayerfully to heaven.
Our ancestors sleep
 in shady groves
amidst granite and marble

while ribbons
of silver rails
and pewter streams
wind through their dreams,
through our lives,
through this town.

Passing Grade

There was a time
we thought
we'd live forever,
never grow old
with skin
like butterflies wings
and strength
to go all day,
all night.
Then,
life held class,
and we,
we learned at her feet
and one by one
earned our diplomas.

Something New Every Day

Buttons and zippers and Velcro,
Oh my!
Little hands learning
to zip and to tie.
Lunchbox and thermos and backpack
Oh dear!
So heavy to carry
my poor little dear.
Colouring, reading and writing,
Oh no!
Then you find out
every day you must go.
Recess and lunch time and classes
Good grief!
Life was so simple
when Mom was the chief.
Homework and notes and letters to home
Sigh!
It's as hard on Mom
as the little guy.

I Remain

I am gone
but no
not forgotten.

I am gone
but here
all the same.

In your smile
I live
in remembrance.

In the sound
of your laughter
I remain.

In the eyes
of our daughter
in the smile
of our son

I remain.

The Fountain of Youth

I've exfoliated, moisturized
spackled and primed
concealed, used blusher
more paint than a mime
tried collagen and q-ten
but sadly my dears
despite all my efforts
I've run out of time
there's not enough product
on my drug store shelf
it's time to give up
on renewing myself
my pocket book's empty
my bank account too
I'm not looking younger
I'm just feeling blue

Julie Kemp Pick

Julie received high praise by her second grade teacher for her story, *My Mommy's My Best Friend.* The writer almost didn't graduate from high school, because she was always late to her 8 a.m. gym class. The bravest thing she's ever done is take her mom to the beauty shop in the rain. Julie's been married for twenty-seven years, and attributes it all to her hard of hearing husband. They have two grown sons: one who encourages her to write more often, the other who encourages her to stock the fridge more often.

Julie's written short stories in *Overcoming Adversity, and East On Central.*

Her blog emptynestinsider.blogspot.com often features her best friend Mom, who in her own words,"...has never been, and will never be a burden."

Wise Revisions

Writing helps connect the dots,
That open worlds of wonder.
Reading in between the lines,
Turn clear skies into thunder.

Waiting for the inspiration,
Sequestered in a silent rage.
Staring at an empty screen,
Wishing words upon the page.

Suddenly the switch turns on,
While ideas churn like butter.
At last the curse is lifted,
As butterflies converge to flutter.

Plagued by second thoughts,
Weary of a cool reception.
Any hopes of turning heads,
Are fueled by misconceptions.

Regrets I have many,
Nervous twitches I have but few.
If only I had begun at twenty,
Should-haves adhere to me like glue.

The phone rings, changing tones,
There's talk of staging a tour.
My hair, my shoes, what will I say?
Thank goodness, I'm not insecure.

The Dope On Online Dating

It started on a dating site,
Wounds still healing from divorce.
She wanted to take things nice and slow,
Let nature take its course.

He wooed her with witty emails,
Courted her with thoughtful texts,
She was virtually swept off her feet,
Wondering what would happen next.

The date was set, the time, the place,
They were finally meeting face to face.
She fussed with her hair, put on a curvaceous
dress,
She waited in anticipation, of the first
impression test.

She wore her heart on her well-toned sleeve,
Her inner beauty, he would never know,
All the plans they made together,
Based on the premise, he would show.

Ode To "T"

Trample on my heart,
Trespass on my soul.
Twisting our love apart,
Tragedy takes its toll.

Trips we'd never take
Trails we'd never follow
Treaties cool, half-baked
Tender tones, are only borrowed.

Tales of days long past,
Trigger tears of sorrow.
Truth is, it would never last,
Trapped inside the treachery of tomorrow.

The Visitor

Visiting Versailles on his Vespa,
Versace clad with favorite boy in tow.
Van heading right in their direction,
Vladie didn't feel a thing from his throw.

Veins pumping full of medications,
Valium surging through the mighty drip.
Vaccines wouldn't really make a difference,
Valleys high and low were on his trip.

Vilmer still reported missing,
Villagers searched throughout the land.
Venom plagued his inner being,
Variable fates for his right hand man.

Veronica pleaded his forgiveness,
Vixen swore she couldn't see a thing.
Valor was something that he stood for,
Velcro kept him seated atop a doughnut ring.

Voice muted as he tried to whisper,
Vanquished of the sounds that dripped like
honey.
Victoriously recovered whole but fractured,
Ventriloquist smiled as words flowed from his
dummy.

Summer Swan Song

The days are getting shorter,
The house has lost its zest.
Everything is now in order,
Though I'd rather have the mess.

No more waiting up all night,
Grateful for what the cat dragged in.
Check-out time is after midnight,
Wondering if I'll ever see my car again.

Lakeside walks, playful lollygagging
The smell of delicious barbecue fills the air.
Wishing I hadn't wasted precious time nagging,
As their memories would be held so dear.

Summer ales, ailing hearts plead for its return,
The boys are quickly growing into men.
The sun is fading, yet it stings the burn,
My husband is stuck alone with me again.

Jilted In July

Jim's jalopy stalled outside the joint,
Jukebox playing their favorite tune.
Juleps ordered at the bar,
Jumpy as he waited for his June.

Jitterbug contest just announced,
Jessie gestured for Jim to take her hand.
Jovial as he politely declined,
Jealous he refused to be her man.

Jaws dropped as men eyed the sultry stranger,
June ran into his outstretched arms.
Jim felt like time stood still,
Joyful as he drank in all her charms.

Jilted Jessie aimed to pull the trigger,
Jigsaw pieces scattered in the hall.
Janitor swept up what was remaining,
Jury's still out on the final call.

Jaywalking en route to the courthouse,
June awaits the trial's outcome.
Judge tenses as June is handcuffed,
Justice served for buying Jessie's gun.

Frequent Flatulence

Frequent Flatulence
Never stood a chance.
Urgently erupting,
Loudly in your pants.

Friendly Fellows,
Meet up at the zoo.
Frolic at the ape house,
Takes the blame off you.

Frequent Flatulence,
Darn digestive tract.
Struggle with momentum,
Before the next attack.

Fancy Footwork,
To the nearest loo.
Carry extra undies,
One pair just won't do.

Friday Function,
At the old age home.
Through aromatic hallways,
Unsuspecting you may roam.

Frequent Flatulence,
Trying to look cool.
What's that floating near you?
Better leave the pool.

Thank You, Angela Lansbury

As a teenager I was Farrah,
All hair and teeth.
Without her curvaceous appeal,
Barely covered underneath.

In college, some called me Stefanie Powers,
Which would've been very high praise,
If only she wasn't vast approaching,
My mother's middle age.

At fifteen I looked twenty,
At twenty I looked thirty.
The harder I tried to shine,
The more I just looked dirty.

Then I saw an Angela Lansbury movie,
She looked old when she was young.
As time went on I noticed,
How her aging gracefully had begun.

Miss Lansbury looks grand at nearly ninety,
Which sets my hopes sky high.
This makes me seriously consider,
Giving reverse aging a try.

For now I'll just keep working,
On being comfortable in my own skin.
By stretching and pulling together,
Attempting to stave off multiple chins.

Goodbye Farrah and Stefanie,
It was fun while it lasted.
Elements have taken their toll,
Which has left me flabbergasted.

Humidity is my kryptonite,
Rendering me powerless to win.
The last time I was caught in it,
I looked like Gary Busey's twin.

Pilgrimage To Grandma's

They were supposed to go to Grandma's for
Thanksgiving,
But the blizzard came in fast.
They tried starting up their snowplow,
It was no use without gas.

Mama quickly gathered supplies,
To fashion homemade skis.
She brought back greasy chopsticks,
So they could zigzag through the trees.

The children created their own goggles,
With paper clips and transparent tape.
This would surely help them navigate,
Through their blustery escape.

Papa loaded up an empty carton,
Filled with lots of delicious treats.
Including some of Grandma's favorites,
To be gobbled at the feast.

They tied it up with shoelace,
And pulled it with a string.
As they skied down the hillside,
With the grace of soaring wings.

She dropped the pencil with a start,
As her mom barged into her room.
"Time to get ready sweetheart,
Grandma will be here soon."

After her jiggly-necked grandma strutted over,
The family all gathered around the stable.
Thankful that they survived another year,
From not being served up on the table.

Between Mothers & Daughters

You took care of us as babies,
Now we're taking care of you.
No ifs, ands, or maybes,
It's what good daughters do.

We try to do our best,
As you always told us to.
Still you put us to the test,
And threaten we'll be through.

Determined to take a stand,
Though a walker is your guide.
No, you will not take my hand,
Something about foolish pride.

Then it all disappears,
When you relay a funny story.
Out pour the happy tears,
Seeing you in all your glory.

You haven't lost your looks,
And your mind is never dense.
That's why I'll let you off the hook,
For telling jokes at my expense.

A Pair To Remember

Flap, flap, flap,
Driving to the store.
Where's my grocery list?
I'll be back for more.

Flap, flap, flap,
I've lost my phone again.
I thought I left it upstairs,
Better check the den.

Flap, flap, flap,
Hurrying to the gym,
Wait, I don't belong here,
Look at the shape I'm in.

Flap, flap, flap,
What's that actor's name?
He was in that silly movie,
This is driving me insane.

Flap, flap, flap,
"Do you hear that flapping, ma?"
"Well, I wasn't gonna say anything,
But you forgot to wear a bra."

Higher Learning

She looked off into the distance,
Deep in thought for what lies ahead.
She fought off the resistance,
As I yanked her out of bed.

Why did things have to change?
She was happy back at home.
Plagued by piercing nervous pangs,
As her imagination began to roam.

She was new to her surroundings,
Most of her friends had gone away.
In a sea of self-doubt she was drowning,
While I reassured her it would be okay.

After I helped her settle in,
She looked up at me betrayed,
As if I tore her from her humble origins,
To be thrust in the wilderness as prey.

Suddenly, a welcoming committee of her peers,
Invited her to join them for dinner.
She discreetly wiped away her tears,
As she waved goodbye to me a winner.

When I turned to close the door,
Alas she hugged me all forgiving.
By her side, as she glided down the floor,
Introducing me to her new friends in assisted
living.

Liza Carens Salerno

Liza Carens Salerno writes from her bones. A freelance writer, blogger and developing fiction writer, she spent a lifetime in the corporate world before a job-elimination forced a long-awaited change in priorities. The next morning words broke out, and she's never looked back. Liza blogs at *Middlepassages-lcs.com*. Her freelance stories and essays have appeared in the *Boston Globe Magazine, South Shore Living,* and *Adoptive Families* Magazines. In a recent blog post, she wrote, "There are times in life emotion is so great, it's hard to express it. That's what poetry is for."

Beginning Color

Dying trees
light the match—
bring first flame
to wood.
Skeleton fingers
rake the sky,
poke holes in
autumn grey.
Mostly though,
they bleed.
Leach red
to orange,
yellow,
you can almost hear
a settled sigh
before they
spark,
flint to rags
of faded green.
Stronger trees pause—

then follow.

Alone at the Beach

Terry cloth sounds,
an old man
turning down
his hearing aid,
mouths like fish,
swallowing
currents of air.
Children splash
with treble mutterings,
little radios
keeping company to
your empty house,
a bleating gull,
music from
the ice cream truck,
all dampened
by the wall
you've fashioned
around yourself,
the only real noise,
a vacuum throb and push,
the wash of blood
pulsing through
your inner ear.

Between Stations

Brakes hiss, trees slip,
Belly-dancing marshes,
chain-link ribbons,
stuttering suns,
bottle-brush pines,
blue-washing maples,
sky-painted ponds,
white birch,
scrub oaks,
backyards—
inflatable pools;
swing-sets,
bikes,
decks,
tunnel,
clatter,
dark,
out,
smoke-stack,
red lights,
crossing gates,
idled traffic,
feathered Sumacs
slowing fences,
couplings thump
asphalt steaming,
mirrors glinting,
air brakes squealing,
engine exhaling,
trembling, stilling and—   Home

A Picture

Outside,
the air strums like a guitar,
rings like a bell.
The weight of a butterfly
starts a yellow-eyed
daisy bobbing—
a fat bee bounces off
the screened back door.
Yesterday,
I watched a tan rabbit
hop from the woods
to the bell-flower patch
lining the garden.
He sniffed the air,
quivering,
before darting through
the yard to vanish
beyond the thickest hedges.

Lake Waban Patchwork

Rowing from
this seamless beach,
weaving through
the warp and weft of
black-water tapestries,
we glide to an
embroidered cove,
where blueberries hang
on green leaf threads,
staining our fingers,
purpling our tongues,
knitting us into patterns
sewn of vintage things,
lily pads and
stippled light,
the flicker of sun
through mustard passings.

To the Airport

The truck on the bridge
clatters overhead,
like I do on the inside,
bleating tarmac fields,
a rush-hour fugue
tuning at my core.

Lean into the wheel
to the calm of night,
a black-inked road,
mounding and falling,
florescent eyes
boring holes through
thick wool curtains—

Ahead, taillights
slice the darkness,
red incisions
score the dark,
etch a forward trail,
but leave it bleeding,
thick and crimson.

Dogwoods in Early Spring

Flowering trees
lift their trains,
young brides,
wedded to a
pale spring sun.
New maples wave
green-palm hands,
spectators to the dance.
Below the blush
of red oak buds,
a portrait hangs,
crocheted lace curtains,
freeze-framed
against a far horizon.

Low Tide at Little Harbor

Warm taupe widens late summer.
Spare of green,
marsh grass bottle-brushes,
broom a lowering sun.
Plough mud,
that organic punk,
a primal slough,
slurps at sandals,
halts descent to
the diggers
forking into
a brown-sugar bar.

In the Kelly clean of spring
You pray not to arrive here,
to forestall the leach of color,
this antiquing air.
But on the marsh,
the season holds its place,
a breath,
before new becomes old.
A slackening tide.

Amid a muted cicadas' bleat,
August yellows a reminder.
We only recognize
how much we love,
after a long goodbye.

For My Daughter on the Cusp of Twenty

I see in you a two a.m. face.
amber light in a wing-back chair,
the talcum arc of rounded cheeks,
coils of love vining an invisible wire.
I had yet to know we all remain infants.
Even as we grey, life casts us
into washing machine blizzards,
snapping limbs,
Marathon bombs, and such.
How to explain—
In some way, you will always feel
two, or seven or ten or nineteen.

At eighty-one my father said
he didn't feel different
until he looked in the mirror.
Now I understand.
I sit on the contoured cushion
of that aging chair,
while down a narrow hallway,
you sleep, folded into yourself
like a moth turned toward the wall.
We are bound now, by compound steel,
And while nothing is the same,
nothing changes.
I know only that
you remain every age you ever were
on the path toward what you'll be,
your nineteen as young as fifty-four,
twenty as old as my ninety-three.

113

Ocular Spring

the windows are dirty.
But still, low in the sky,
a silver-sun
cleans the edges,
the world sprayed
with Windex,
polished hard
with a soft felt cloth.
Out in the garden,
emerging stalks
etch blue air,
green leaves outlined
in fine-point ink,
like the first time
you don a
pair of glasses,
the new prescription
cuts a sharp line.

Later in the car,
you lumber down
winter-pocked roads,
amid strobes
flicking and flashing
light
hits air,
hits trees
hits air.
You adjust the visor lower,
reach for a baseball cap,
anything to block

the brash blaze of
horizon glare,
before trees leaf out,
tint the bleach
with shade.
You squint as
back-light marries
a white magnolia,
branches hanging heavy,
the way limbs do
during a wet spring snow.

Tomorrow, the light will change.
A storm that never arrived,
but washed the air anyway,
will have floated out to sea.
All you'll have left
of an afternoon
burnished to
a high-gloss shine,
are words that try —
reminding you, perhaps,
but failing to capture
anything close to
the essence.

Late March Morning

We wake to snow
grey light and
worsted wool suiting,
draped across a table,
pillows plumped on
Adirondack chairs,
white climbing a ladder,
left out from weekend chores.
Birdhouses pose
in caps knitted by
a grandmother,
and all around,
bushes bend
at the waist,
grouped men bowing,
invoking pardon from
this winter's God.

A Salad Poem

You dream the aroma
of a ripe tomato,
the twist and snap and green smell
of vine and sun-warmed hands.
It's all there in the seed,
or sapling bedded in loam.
You count forward-time,
hot days and long months,
until the plant hangs heavy,
a bowl returns full,
until you slice and salt
and pair
with half-moons of
oozing cheese,
knee-buckling at
the sweet, hot swallow
of acid
and saliva.
It's all there,
as you tear open the package.
sprinkle the seeds.
Press them into egg carton cups.
A repository for summer,
an incubator of earth to mouth,
a sauce, a salsa, a sandwich.
You brush dirt over with your finger,
and feel the promise of wait.

Finale

Since fall
the news has weighed
like a nugget, a stone,
a shard of glass,
bloodying
the inside of a shoe.

In winter
you hoped the wind
screaming at shutters
would snatch it, bury it
drop it into an
anonymous sea.

But always—
Snows melt.
Oceans rise.

By spring
we speak of dogwood brides,
the pink lava of phlox pouring
over granite ledge,
the return of hummingbirds
levitating at the window—

By May
blossoms knit
hand to thread,
Bradford Pears, Magnolias,
the crisp call of a song sparrow
high in the trees.

But this year it births
choked words,
unyielding frost,
a prediction.
Every season after,
uninhabited.
Still.

Susan Flett Swiderski

Susan was born and raised in Dundalk,
Maryland, where everybody calls everybody *hon*,
fishing and crabbing is a way of life, and eating
steamed crabs is practically a sacrament. She
and her husband moved to Georgia so many
years ago, they practically qualify as natives, and
even though she truly loves living in the Peach
State, part of her heart will always linger up
north on the sweet shores of the Chesapeake
Bay. With their children grown and married and
their grandchildren growing entirely too fast,
she and her hubby currently share their home
with two spoiled cats, Dot and Dash. Weird
names, perhaps, but not for a couple of amateur

120

radio operators. Susan and her husband, that is. Not the cats.

Her previous work includes pieces published in *World Radio* and *Woman's World* magazines, and her debut novel *Hot Flashes and Cold Lemonade,* which can be found on Amazon. She also blogs more or less weekly at www.susan.swiderski.blogspot.com

Now that *Old Broads* has been launched, she hopes to begin work on her next novel… just as soon as her cats move their hairy butts from the front of her computer screen.

A Necessary Change in Nomenclature

He used to call me Hot Rod
Many years ago;
Why he picked a name so odd,
I honestly don't know.

I wasn't very *fast* at all,
Though my lines were sleek and trim;
My engine wasn't one to stall,
And my lights were never dim.

My perky rack was rather small,
And my o-pinions, smart and sassy;
I wasn't *fast*... as I recall...
But I had a creak-free chassis.

Now, my joints could use some lube,
And my body, an overhaul;
Maybe some bondo in my left boob,
And a paint job over all.

My exhaust may sometimes backfire,
And I often run out of go,
But the situation ain't so dire,
Because one thing I know:
Of all his cars, his fave of all
Is a Model A, you see,
That '30 gal is a *rat rod*...
And an awful lot like me!

The Ungrateful Cat

'Twas one in the morning, I vow,
When I heard a cat meow from a bough.
High up in a tree,
He seemed helpless to me.
Begged I, "Please get him down now."

With a frown, my man gave a cough,
Said, "No need to get the cat off.
He made his way up;
He can make his way down."
And I batted my eyes, sure enough.

'Twas sleeting and icy, so rough,
But my sweetie, so tender, so tough,
Climbed up on our ladder,
But that didn't matter;
To the cat, it wasn't enough.

The cat pulled back out of reach;
My man yelled, "Son of a beech!"
He stretched a bit more
To the kitty so poor,
And the cat gave a God-awful screech.

'Twas dark, so I couldn't quite see,
But the cat came tearing past me.
He'd run down my sweetie
And clawed off some meatie,
So I figured in trouble I'd be.

"No more!" my man roared to me.
"Next time, we leave the cats be.
We don't need no damned ladder;
It just doesn't matter.
Have you e-ver... seen bones... in a tree?"

Learning to Fly

A short walk from my Nana's house
Was a most exciting place:
An aging playground with a two-story slide
And swings that could reach the sky.
Mighty chains hung from a massive frame,
The tallest you ever saw,
And the standing dare for every kid there
Was to spin a swing all the way 'round.

One day in May, I raced to a swing,
Determined to beat that dare;
Amid cheers and jeers, I parked my rear
And launched myself into the air.
I pumped my legs harder and harder still;
The chains, they creaked and moaned.
But I hung on tight with all my might,
And soared higher and higher still.

I leaned back, kicked high,
And pulled back on the chain,
With my ponytail flying, and my cousins crying,
"Go, Susie! You're almost there!"
Then with a forward lean and bended knee,
I flew backwards oh so high.
Wind whistled in my ears and stung my eyes,
But I had to go higher still.

"I've gotta stand," thought my stupid brain,
"And try to pick up speed."
So up I try to get… still flying yet…

125

Not the best plan, you'll soon see.
When I hit the ground, every bit of air
Deserted me with a whoosh.
I couldn't breathe, and I couldn't move,
So I lay motionless in the dirt.

"I knew she couldn't do it," one boy sneered.
"Is she dead?" another one cried.
I lay there bleeding, without breathing,
Wondering myself if I'd died.
Then finally, I wheezed a breath of air,
My lungs screamed in agony;
Then I slowly stood and shook it off,
And reached for the swing again.

I never made that swing go 'round;
No kid ever did;
But many tried, and many cried
Amid the cheers and jeers.
The old frame's still there,
But the swings are gone,
"Not safe," everyone declared,
But I'll never forget, and will cherish long
Those many times that I dared.

Now, I am the Nana,
And my grandkids love to swing
On the playset in their back yard,
And they beg me to push and sing.
"Higher, Grandma!" they yell at me,
But I push with a gentle touch,
Holding back to protect them,
Fearful of pushing too much.

Then I remember the joy of pumping my legs
And flying high on my own,
Wind whistling and stinging my teary eyes,
Feeling strong and unafraid.
I let go of the swing and smile at them
And say, "Give it a try.
Hang on tight and pump your legs!"
Because now's their turn to fly.

This peculiar ditty was written to accompany a blog post about odd medical procedures, in general, and tobacco smoke enemas, in particular:

How to Cure a Cold

A call girl once had a cold
And went to her doctor, I'm told.
He blew smoke up her butt
And into her gut—
In two weeks, she felt good as gold.

Then few called on her for a fling,
For she developed a peculiar thing:
When she coughed or passed gas,
Smoke puffed out her ass
In a perfect, but smelly, smoke ring.

Am I?

Is it horrid to be happy
When so many are so sad;
Is it heartless to be filled with peace
When war's all some have had?
Is it wrong to sing a joyful song
When others live the blues;
Is it crass to count sweet blessings
When some have none to lose?
Is it selfish to eat chocolate cake
When others have no meal;
Is it callous to be healthy
When some will never heal?
Is it hateful to be wrapped in love
When some are all alone;
Is it sinful to leap and pirouette
When others cry and moan?

I lift my arms in gratitude
And admire the morning sun,
Humbled by this gift of life…
Thank God for giving me one!
Yet I know I wield Excalibur
While some hold only air;
Life's a wondrous miracle,
But it isn't always fair.
Is it enough to love our fellow man
And do our best to share;
Is it enough to empathize and pray
And to always to show we care?
It is in some ways troubling
And foolish to pretend;

In light of others' suffering,
I ask of you, my friend ---

Am I heartless to be filled with peace
When war's all some have had;
Am I horrid to be happy
When so many are so sad?

Ode to Old Age

I found a hair there under my chin,
And I yanked that sucker out,
But wouldn't you know, the very next day,
Two more began to sprout.
I don't know what's happening;
It's a perplexing change of pace.
My arms and legs are going bald,
But I have to shave my face.

It's such a rotten travesty;
My tummy once was flat.
But now my hourglass is mostly ass,
And my waist has turned to fat.
My body's slowly sagging,
And I don't look so hot;
If a man wants to ogle my bosom now,
I'm afraid he'll have to squat.

But that's okay, 'cause I'm still here,
Of life I'm still a part.
So what if when I bend or stretch,
I leak a little fart?
I've lots of life and love in store,
Though I'm not young and shiny;
If ya wanta know the truth,
Old age can kiss my heinie.

I wrote the following poem for a blogfest in which participants were to reveal their dream destinations. (Smarticus is the alias I gave my hubby.)

The Perfect Place

Picking a dream destination
Took a heap of contemplation.
Shall I go north, south, east, or west?
Which one place would be the best?

For beauty and wildlife of great wonder,
What land better than the one Down Under?
Bright flowers, koalas, and kangaroos,
And a duck-billed platypus, I'd like to choose.
Plus, while I'm there, know what I'd do?
Visit with a blogger pal or two.

Then, again...

I'd love to see the Northern Lights,
One of Earth's most amazing sights...
A surreal sky of shifting hues,
Of reds, and greens, and electric blues.
So perhaps, it's best when I go forth,
To set the GPS for way up north.

Then, again...

There's Glasgow, London, and Paris, too;
Most any place in Europe would do.

132

What history, culture, and oh... the food!
(If I can't speak their language, will they think
me rude?)
Or maybe Africa to see a jungle beast,
Or perhaps the mysteries of the far far east?

Then, again...

How foolish to run to far-off Tibet
When there's places **here** I haven't seen yet.
Mount Rushmore, Grand Canyon, and Niagara
Falls...
Such beauty to see... and Old Faithful calls!
New England, California, Utah, and Maine,
Buttes, mountains, deserts, glaciers, and plain.

Then, again...

After giving the matter consideration,
What matters isn't destination,
For the dream doesn't spring from a special
place;
It's more about a special face.
Whether we travel far away,
Or in our town we choose to stay,
What matters (although he's sometimes a
farticus),
Is being *wherever* with my guy Smarticus.

I Am

I am from yesterday; from people, places, and
times gone by; from sad memories that sear my
soul, and joyous ones that make me sing…

I am from ocean, bay, river and creek; from Old
Bay seafood seasoning, blue crabs, and
homemade bread pudding made with stale white
bread and rum-soaked raisins.

I am from a row house on a postage stamp lot
in a noisy kid-filled neighborhood; from a tiny
room with paper-thin walls that kept no secrets
and hid no cries; from a squeaky window fan
that sucked in air scented with dog mess and
lilacs.

I am from hula hoops and bob-a-loops,
hopscotch, and hot pink handlebar streamers;
from roller skating in the street, jumping rope in
the alley, and shooting beer bottles in the woods
with a borrowed BB gun.

I am from dandelions and daisies, Black-eyed
Susans, and sweet blankets of deep pink wild
roses; from soil as dark as coffee grounds, fat
earthworms wriggling on a fishhook, and
fireflies twinkling in a jelly jar covered with a
nail-punched lid.

I am from parents with no sense of direction, grandparents who pretended to be stern, and wonderfully silly aunts; from cousins who were friends, and friends who were lifesavers.

I am from singing: with Mitch Miller, in cars, in bars, and around campfires with guitars and bongo drums; from books and more books, Scrabble, and crossword puzzles; from Pinochle, pitching pennies and baseball cards, and rousing games of penny ante poker; from frantic footraces to the mailbox at the end of the street.

I am from today; from husband, children, and the best grandchildren in the world; from embracing new adventures and making new memories that make my heart sing...

I am wife, mother, and oh-so-silly grandmother, with cousins who are still friends, and friends who are still lifesavers; from red clay, dogwood trees and azaleas; from a modest home on a good-sized lot in a quiet neighborhood; from Old Bay seafood seasoning, blue crabs, and bread pudding made with cinnamon swirl raisin bread, and smothered in caramel rum sauce.

I am from books and more books, writing and more writing, crossword puzzles, Scrabble, and Suduko; from blasting bull's-eyes out of targets at the gun club, and walking leisurely to the mailbox at the end of the driveway.

135

I am from yesterday; I am from today; I am an updated still-singing version of the old-fashioned me… and exactly where I'm supposed to be.

I Was There

Kilroy was here.
Frightened,
Hopeful,
Filled with bravado,
I left my mark,
Proving to posterity
That I was there.
Look.
Do you see it?
Do you remember me?
I was there.
And then...
Blown away
By the uncaring winds of time...
I was gone.

Footprints in the sand.
Running,
Playing,
Filled with life,
I left my mark,
Proving to posterity
That I was there.
Look.
Do you see them?
Do you remember me?
I was there.
And then...
Washed away
By the uncaring waves of time...
I was gone.

Bootprints in the snow.
Crunching,
Sliding,
Chilled with cold,
I left my mark,
Proving to posterity
That I was there.
Look.
Do you see them?
Do you remember me?
I was there.
And then...
Melted away
By the uncaring suns of time...
I was gone.

Do you remember me?
Does anybody care?
I was there.
Oh yes,
Once upon a time...
I was there.

A Grandchild's Wish

Fishing with my buddy, that's where I long to
be;
In the early morn, with no one around but the
gulls,
My grandpop,
And me.
Sometimes we'd talk, and sometimes not;
We really wouldn't care.
It would just be wonderful to be together there.
The air so fresh and cool, and the sky all
streaked with light,
We'd bob in our little rented boat and watch the
end of night.
He'd bait my hook without making any fun of
me,
And would listen while I spun my tales of what
I want to be.
We'd be the best of buddies, and everything
would be so right.
To tell the truth, we wouldn't care if the fish
didn't care to bite.
Yes, fishing with my buddy, that's where I long
to be;
In the early morn, with no one around but the
gulls,
My grandpop,
And me.

The End

There are many more days behind me
Than are left for me ahead,
And I know it's inevitable
That too soon, I'll wake up dead.
That prospect doesn't bother me,
But I think it would be great
If my bottom boasted a "best by" stamp
Showing my expiration date.
Now, I'm in no rush to reach my end,
But if that date were clearly seen,
I wouldn't waste my moolah
Buying bananas that are green.

There are many more pages behind you
Than are left for you ahead,
And it's, of course, inevitable
That this book has gotta end.
I'm not going anywhere;
I plan to stay awhile…
But this book's pages are about kaput,
And it's due for the finished pile.
Though its end is drawing nigh,
Resurrection can be your due.
Just turn back to the beginning,
And read it all anew.

ABOUT CARE

Founded in 1945 with the creation of the CARE Package®, CARE is a leading humanitarian organization fighting global poverty. CARE places special focus on working alongside poor girls and women because, equipped with the proper resources, they have the power to lift whole families and entire communities out of poverty. Last year CARE worked in 87 countries and reached more than 97 million people around the world. To learn more, visit www.care.org.

Made in the USA
Charleston, SC
ber 2014